ONCE UPON A DREAM

Whispers Of Dreams

Edited By Lynsey Evans

First published in Great Britain in 2024 by:

Young Writers
Remus House
Coltsfoot Drive
Peterborough
PE2 9BF
Telephone: 01733 890066
Website: www.youngwriters.co.uk

All Rights Reserved
Book Design by Ashley Janson
© Copyright Contributors 2024
Softback ISBN 978-1-83565-503-0
Printed and bound in the UK by BookPrintingUK
Website: www.bookprintinguk.com
YB0592T

FOREWORD

Welcome Reader, to a world of dreams.

For Young Writers' latest competition, we asked our writers to dig deep into their imagination and create a poem that paints a picture of what they dream of, whether it's a make-believe world full of wonder or their aspirations for the future.

The result is this collection of fantastic poetic verse that covers a whole host of different topics. Let your mind fly away with the fairies to explore the sweet joy of candy lands, join in with a game of fantasy football, or you may even catch a glimpse of a unicorn or another mythical creature. Beware though, because even dreamland has dark corners, so you may turn a page and walk into a nightmare!

Whereas the majority of our writers chose to stick to a free verse style, others gave themselves the challenge of other techniques such as acrostics and rhyming couplets.

Each piece in this collection shows the writers' dedication and imagination – we truly believe that seeing their work in print gives them a well-deserved boost of pride, and inspires them to keep writing, so we hope to see more of their work in the future!

CONTENTS

Cotham Gardens Primary School, Cotham

Eric Bourlard-Rodriguez (10)	1
Kamilla Jumakajeva (10)	2
Holly Hart (11)	3
Olive Mae Everett (11)	4
Isla Evans (9)	5
Sahej Singh (10)	6
Chloe Chant (10)	7
Oliver Simons (10)	8
Oscar Clive (10)	9
Lorna Vail Hogg (9)	10
Raviro Walker (11)	11

Dorrington Academy, Birmingham

Anisa Ali (8)	12
Anaika Joshi (9)	13
Adam Elawad (9)	14
Eliza Sajid (8)	15
Rayaan Ashfaq (8)	16
Eliza Hossain (9)	17
Juwairiyah Ayaz (8)	18
Jasmine Agrawal (8)	19
Manya Pathania (8)	20
Amelia Khaliq (9)	21
Amirah Khan (9)	22

Elloughton Primary School, Elloughton

Molly Parkinson (9)	23
Felicity Caley (9)	24

Hanslope Primary School, Hanslope

Ivy Hanson (10)	26

Hillside Avenue Primary And Nursery School, Norwich

Jenson Coulson (8)	27
Abigail Evans (9)	28
Arissa Ali (9)	30
Charlotte Godfrey-Daynes (9)	31
Elika Rafiee (8)	32
Keavy Taylor (9)	33
Zoe Asamoah (8)	34
Sienna Fairall (9)	35

Kingscourt School, Catherington

Georgia Morphett (11) & Grace	36
Tabby George (11) & Orla	39
Charter (11)	
Cecilia Banning (11)	40
Lara Pitcher (11)	42
Imogen Bartlett (10)	43

Lark Hall Primary School, Lambeth

Haroun Bassour (8)	44

Lower Darwen Primary School, Lower Darwen

Bonnie Holden (8)	45

Jessica Cottam (11) & Sienna Holden (11)&46
Jessica Briggs (11)&47
Rosie Hayes (10)&48
Gracie Wilson (9)&49
Aizah Qureshi (9)&50
Adam Patel (10)&51
Elza Bachare (10)&52
Austin Davis (9)&53
Olivia Rogers (8)&54
Katie Nightingale (9)&55
Logan Lewis (10), Theodore Orrell (10) & William Murphy (10)&56
Esta Mason-Tabbinor (8)&57
Alfie Montague (10)&58
Freya Eccles (10)&59
Phoebe Hibbert (8)&60

Moor End Community Primary School, Oswaldtwistle

Monica Ruggieri (8)&61
Harper Taylor (9)&62
Elsa Taylor (9)&63
Catelyn O'Rourke (9)&64
Lachlan Mclennan (8)&65
Sarim Ali Hashmi (9)&66
Oscar Speight (8)&67
Skylar Shaw (9)&68
Eric Allen (8)&69
Ruby Clarke (8)&70
Alaena Whyte (9)&71
Sophie Beeston (9)&72
Asa Solch (9)&73
Cody Long (9)&74

Newbridge Primary School, Bath

Ollie Attah (9)&75
Jake Snook (10)&76
Cerys Little (10)&77
Isla Stacey (10)&78
Elsa Wicks (10)&79
Isobel Manners (10)&80

Eli Robertson (9)&81
Henry Navias (9)&82

Nicholas Hawksmoor Primary School, Towcester

Mia Gowling (8)&83
Seiki Komatsu (9)&85

Okehampton Primary School And Foundation Unit, Okehampton

Max Drew (8)&87
Zuzanna Krzysiek (7)&88
Kensi Pettis (8)&90
Hetty Stevens (7)&91
Paige Baily (7)&92
Lyla Gibbs (8)&93

Ormiston Meadows Academy, Peterborough

Fareeha Memon (8)&94

Outwood Primary Academy Kirkhamgate, Kirkhamgate

Evelyn Geary (8)&95
Harry Robinson (8)&96

Ribbon Academy, Murton

Leila-May Lugg (7)&97
Cora Smith (8)&98
Gracie Purvis (8)&100
Victoria Ann Byles (8)&102
Freddie Pinder (8)&104
Theo Fawcett (8)&106
Ava Florence Emmerson (7)&108
Robert Charlton (8)&110
Kai Johnson (8)&112
Courtney Wilkinson (8)&114
Caiden Adams (8)&116
Lynkon Spooner (7)&118
Jacobjohn Self (7), Christopher & Great&119

Harper 120
Wyatt Ball (7) 121
Lucy Newton (7) 122
Zak 123

Seend CE Primary School, Seend

Darcey Corbett (7) 124
Rose Freegard (8) 125
Chloe Grabham (7) 126
Faye Long (8) 127

St Bride's Primary School, Belfast

Nuha Jasrul Azily (9) 128
Evelina Khaidanova (8) 129

St Christopher's RC Primary School, Ashton-Under-Lyne

Theo Mason-Diamond (10) 130
Sofia Gabrane (11) 132
Jessica Thompson (11) 134
Elise Foronda (10) 136
Tadek Chmara (10) 137
Aleesha Abraham (11) 138
Nevil Jishore Thuruthen (10) 139
Layla Boardman (11) 140
Harper Thompstone (10) 141

St George's Bickley CE Primary School, Bromley

Kornelia Kovtun (8) 142
Georgina Johnson (8) 143
Isobel Richards (8) 144
Emil Kasymbekov (9) 145
Edie Ward (8) 146

St John Vianney's Catholic Primary School, Blackpool

Shivam Shukla (10) 147
Rebecca Bartrupe (11) 148
Julia Foniok (11) 149
Jack Kelly (10) & Olivia 150

St Matthew's C of E Primary School, West Wimbledon

Calla Bliss Rayne (8) 151
Elizabeth Worth (10) 152
Apolline Boursier (8) 154
Caitie Thompson (11) 155
Edward Jarman (8) 156
Kayan Bansoodeb (8) 157
Ben Grogan (11) 158
Sylvia Carey (8) 159

St Thomas Of Canterbury RC Primary School, Salford

László Hüse (10) 160
Christina Matova (9) 162
Iwinosa Gabbrellia (8) 163
Horiya Azid (8) 164
Dexter Obasogie (9) 166
Hannan Albath (10) 167
Thomas Donley (9) 168
Samina Haji (10) 169
Ayat Uddin (9) 170
Lana Khoshnaw (8) 171
Therese Mendy (8) 172
Sharon Eze (9) 173
Elim Frezgi (9) 174

THE POEMS

THE POEMS

Dreams

Dreams?
What are dreams?
Some are scary,
Full of fright,
Of bats and spiders in the night.
Some are joyful,
Full of delight,
Of lollipops and candyfloss in the light.
Some are heroic,
With battles to brave,
Of princesses in towers, ready to save.
Some are wizards,
Casting some spells,
And of enchanted wishing wells.
Some are of boats,
Going into the fray,
Of powerful sea beasts, yet to slay.
And once you wake,
From your good night's sleep,
You think to yourself, *is my dreaming complete?*

Eric Bourlard-Rodriguez (10)
Cotham Gardens Primary School, Cotham

1

In My Dream

In my dream I appear in Candyland
Lollipop trees, candyfloss bushes, gummy plants and
biscuit butterflies
Until it's dark, I'm somewhere else
Skies red, eagles screech and the trees are towering
above me, I don't like it here anymore
The ocean appears; fish swimming, coral swaying, the
water blue
The sea changes to a shimmering forest
Fairies fly, elves scatter and glitter shines before falling
to the soft, mossy ground
It's over, the dream's over, I'm in my bed thinking
What will I dream tomorrow? Who knows.

Kamilla Jumakajeva (10)
Cotham Gardens Primary School, Cotham

A Cave Of Crystals

I stumbled upon a crystal cave
It sounded like a crazy rave
I crawled inside to take a peek
Instead, I found a mutated leek
He showed me the way to the main event
I ended up underneath a tent
There were pixies and ponies
There was pizza and macaroni
Above me was a giant disco ball
Reflecting off the rainbow crystal
Suddenly, all the noise stopped
My dream disappeared with a *pop*
I wake up in my cosy bed
With the memory of the dream in my head.

Holly Hart (11)
Cotham Gardens Primary School, Cotham

Sweet Like Summer

Summer is sweet,
Sweet like cake,
Like a fresh apple pie ready to bake,
Chocolate, coconut, pineapples and more,
Cupcakes, pastries, puddings galore,
So many options, but which one to choose,
Maybe I can hide a cake or two in my shoes,
Summer is sweet,
Like a treat,
Like sugar,
Like ice cream,
Or ice tea,
So look, summer is sweet,
From its hot weather to its cool drinks,
Summer is the best, wink, wink.

Olive Mae Everett (11)
Cotham Gardens Primary School, Cotham

The Darkness

Tall trees tower above me
Monsters cower in the shadows
My only company is the darkness
It can't talk but it can listen
The trees rustle with the force of the wind
And the monsters come out of the shadows
The mud beneath my feet starts to dry
The urge of wanting to turn
To run
The wind begins to soften
I feel my body calm
The rain begins to fall
Pitter, patter
And I return to my living self.

Isla Evans (9)
Cotham Gardens Primary School, Cotham

Tackled

Crowds cheering,
People betting,
But more people in Reading,
The game's beginning,
Ronaldo shooting,
Alisson Becker blocking,
Haaland defending,
Uh, now Messi faking,
But the unexpected comes to life,
No more people flying kites,
He shoots, he scores,
Sui!
Wait, is this all just a dream?

Sahej Singh (10)
Cotham Gardens Primary School, Cotham

Corn Dogs

In my dreams...
Flying among giant corn dogs
With friends
Oh, soaring around
Beyond the clouds
The corn dogs begin to fade
The dream's nearly gone!
What shall I do?
Snuggle down and down some more
And they come back!
Me and my friends breathe a sigh of relief
Phew.
I eat a corn dog.

Chloe Chant (10)
Cotham Gardens Primary School, Cotham

Winter

W inter, cold fun in the snow
I n our hearts, hope for snow
N ight lit, I see snow, bursting with joy
T ight in bed, waiting for the morning
E merald light shines down
R un, run, as fast as you can, to the horse shed. Ride
into the sun.

Oliver Simons (10)
Cotham Gardens Primary School, Cotham

Once Upon A Dream, There Was A Star

A star glimmering hopefully in a vast expanse of black,
The end of the colour bar.
A dream, radiating joy.
The thought of a world,
A world swirled with smiles,
The floor, no war, paved with dreams,
Glowed bright like a fat yellow bee.

Oscar Clive (10)
Cotham Gardens Primary School, Cotham

I've Never Dreamt Since

I've never dreamt since
Red skies
Nightmares unfold
My blood
Runs cold
My heart
Twist tense
My home
No defence
This phoenix
Didn't rise
I've never dreamt since.

Lorna Vail Hogg (9)
Cotham Gardens Primary School, Cotham

Waldo

W earily glancing,
A re they here yet?
L ightheadedness hits me,
D eath comes looming in,
O ver. They found Waldo.

Raviro Walker (11)
Cotham Gardens Primary School, Cotham

Butterflies

B utterflies fly across the glamorous glowing moon
L ittle waves fill the magical blue sea
U nique butterflies fill the dark night sky
E legantly dance through the night.

B utterflies are as blue as the planet Neptune
U pon the magical, mystical blue sea
T railing across the glowing moon
T rusting their wings to keep them above the sea
E legantly fly in the sky
R evealing their true beauty
F lying upon the sea
L ightly fluttering plant to plant
I ncredible wings
E legant
S pecial to me.

Anisa Ali (8)
Dorrington Academy, Birmingham

Nightmares Happen

N othing has prepared me for this land, I see,

I n the gloomy haunted house, as scary as can be.

G reen, gloomy eyes appear in smoke,

H ow did I get here? Is this all a joke?

T *hud!* Something moves,

M y worst fear is released: a creepy dragon!

A fire-breathing dragon, ahh! Blazing fire like a scorching volcano,

R unning as fast as I can go.

E yes are glowsticks that burst wide open,

S uddenly, I found myself at my bedside, realising it was a dream.

Anaika Joshi (9)
Dorrington Academy, Birmingham

The Lost Astronaut

A lost astronaut,
S earching the galaxy,
T o find a way home,
R acing through space like speeding cars,
O ver the stars that glisten like diamonds, hundreds of planets stroll through the Milky Way
N owhere near Earth,
A ll around the galaxy they go,
U ntil he finds his one and only home,
T umbling to Earth when suddenly it's just a dream.

Adam Elawad (9)
Dorrington Academy, Birmingham

Wonderland

W hite sparkling snow is near,

O n days, we hop and cheer.

N ever-ending fun,

D reams are like floating colourful cartoons in your mind,

E very star is so bright.

R eady for the marvellous midnight,

L ove spreads everywhere,

A mazing toys, no need to share.

N ever want a frown on my face,

D on't want to leave this place!

Eliza Sajid (8)
Dorrington Academy, Birmingham

My Aspiration

D iverging pathways, but only one leads to my aspiration.

R ewarded for caring for people, will be my profession.

E very winter, microbes scurrily jump into patients' immune systems.

A ctions are taken after patients display depressing symptoms.

M edical NHS team are working immensely here.

S oon after taking miraculous medicines, patients joyfully cheer.

Rayaan Ashfaq (8)
Dorrington Academy, Birmingham

Me And The World

D azzling in the forest,

R eady to have an adventure,

E ager, dreadful dragons ready to pounce like a tiger getting his prey,

A s I drifted across the room in my beautiful, breathtaking dress, everyone gasped at me,

M ajestic unicorns galloped through the sunny, gorgeous fields,

S parkling, gorgeous fairies leave a glowing trail behind them.

Eliza Hossain (9)
Dorrington Academy, Birmingham

Monsters In The Night

M orning to night, not in the light
O n the dark moon but not so bright
N ot so good, but not so bad
S cary, sneaky beasts appear in the night
T hat monster stays every night
E verywhere is the monster's realm
R ight here, right now
S tay in bed until it's dead.

Juwairiyah Ayaz (8)
Dorrington Academy, Birmingham

The Magical Ring

D own there in the spooky, secret forest, a ring catches my eye,

R ight there in front of me, a light shone,

E verything went black as I took the glistening ring off.

A s everything began to disappear, I said to myself, amazing.

M y family being happy was the best thing I saw. I woke up.

Jasmine Agrawal (8)
Dorrington Academy, Birmingham

Fairies

F airies, I found in my room,
A round the room with a broom,
I didn't believe what I found,
R ight to left and making a singing sound,
I joined their singing and fun,
E very fairy had to run,
S omehow, something woke me up with the beautiful,
shining sun.

Manya Pathania (8)
Dorrington Academy, Birmingham

Untitled

D andelions falling in a forest full of flowers,
R umbling trees in a forest full of trees,
E lephant floating upside down.
A ir breathing rapidly, running through the forest,
M onkeys dancing.

Amelia Khaliq (9)
Dorrington Academy, Birmingham

Where The Golden Ticket Takes Me

Chocolate-coated fun,
Makes imagination run.
Sugar covered bliss;
The gummy bears dancing around,
Candy canes grow like flowers.

Amirah Khan (9)
Dorrington Academy, Birmingham

Dreams Beyond Me

I haven't fallen into a dream before, I wonder what it's like.

M agic every step you take no matter where you go

A liens dancing on the table

G iant monsters making a sound every step

I haven't fallen into a dream before I wonder what it's like.

N othing can stop me from dancing with aliens

A liens are talking, I wonder why.

T errible pirates are sailing a boat

I n the water is a wizard, I wonder why.

O n this adventure, I make some new friends too

N othing will stop me from loving this world.

Molly Parkinson (9)
Elloughton Primary School, Elloughton

The Hummingbird And The Kingfisher

F inally, in my dreams in this land I see

R oaming animals, hiding in the deepest depths where I be.

I n case of an emergency, I step back, but I hear a flutter of wings far ahead -

E nvy and glory, the bird felt sick. So he fled to a faraway bed where he slept there all night.

N ightfall rose, all around them, a bright flash of light caught his eye

D ominoes fell - except the big tree

S torming, striking as loud as can be,

H ere stood a little ladybird, beautiful as can be,

I t stood there strong and looked like a hummingbird.

P inched and picked, they heard a crash and the tree went down.

M eaning the hummingbird saved his life from the old, brown tree.

E ver and ever from that tree on,

A rrange and adapt, they became friends.

N ever again will it happen because the two of them stay in their own brown hut

S eeing ships and birds soaring by.

E very day, everywhere, they travel to somewhere new

V ultures, penguins to Peru.

E very evening in London, they see Paddington Bear,

R attling shakers and hiding in a bin.

Y ears go by

T hey soar up high.

H e taught himself to breathe underwater,

I even got taught how to do a summersault,

N ight, toasting nice bugs by the fire,

G ardening, cleaning, but there's no place like Cosy. Little. Home.

Felicity Caley (9)
Elloughton Primary School, Elloughton

My Little Fantasy

I stand, my billowing dress of blue,
In a forest of daisies so bold and true.
Upon my head is a crown of daisies,
My vision still blurred and still so hazy.
I skip towards the tree,
My curiosity getting the better of me.
I settle down on a picnic blanket,
Quietly awaiting my filling banquet.
When my banquet does not come,
A sweet little tune I do hum.
My cheeks, a colour of rosy red,
Locks of bouncing ringlets upon my head.
I lie back softly, admiring the view,
And piano music plays as if on cue.
I smile, a smile so incredibly bright,
A smile so gentle it could banish the night.
Colourful daisies here and there,
An eternal field of them, not a single scare.
I stand up and begin to flee,
My dream becoming a reality.
And that's all about my little fantasy.

Ivy Hanson (10)
Hanslope Primary School, Hanslope

Misery Nightmares

M ight be scary but behind me when I look right

I nto my wardrobe, it stares... with giant eyes looking

S traight towards me he started chasing but he couldn't

E xactly catch me, immediately I got lost... "Where?"

R ight in front of me is Harry at least, a dragon swooped in

Y ikes but we were in Fairy and Unicorn Land where we were safe

k **N** ights came racing past us but they were shape-shifters

I nterestingly and then a wizard comes into our

G roup and his name is Zolon which I think is cool

H opefully, the clowns aren't bad but this one is bad like

T he Savage World. It's dreadful, "It's in here!" Races

M adly towards us and Matai is here now with beady eyes

A nnoyingly we all jumped on our pet dragon and he

R aced like a bomb, he upgrades, even worse when he

E rupts as loud as possible, when he grabs me and...

S uddenly I woke up and it was just a nightmare...

Jenson Coulson (8)
Hillside Avenue Primary And Nursery School, Norwich

Pirates Coming In

Absolutely nothing is more terrifying than this -
Dragons sway from side to side, breathing fire as light
darkens
Swiftly, we all stay in one cramped space
Then I realise there's a pirate ship following us
Is there nothing more scary than this?
Everyone shivers but I don't
I just stand there, watching whales swim nervously
Feeling panicked, I rushed to the top deck of the
mighty ship
They are obviously looking for some new slaves who
could possess nothing.

A beam glances above the ship
That means that we are nearly on land
But with a pirate ship behind us we're doomed
How on Earth is this enjoyable when we might die
soon?
Like I wish we had some weapons like a razor-sharp
sword
Something like that
All that I know is that I would not sail this wealthy,
expensive, luxurious ship
I knew that everyone was terrified

There was nothing that I could do
I couldn't only shoot arrows
Hopefully, that will work
It did, what a glorious day!

Abigail Evans (9)
Hillside Avenue Primary And Nursery School, Norwich

The Ballerina Unicorn

Prancing, dancing everywhere in my dreams
I see rainbow hair twirling to and fro
In my mind, your horn will blow,
Mighty and bold, clear and strong
I can hear a beautiful song,
Riding, gliding light as a feather,
Clip clop, clip clop, here I come,
Sparkling, twinkling just like a star
Twisting, turning, see me spin,
Flying, flying way up high
Soaring, diving in the moonlit sky,
Leaping, jumping, tail up high
Galloping, galloping, twist and fly,
Scattering, clattering, love everywhere
Ducking and swerving, clinging on with hooves
Dancing to the well-known groove,
Sliding, bending, moving to the beat
"Come on sleepyhead let's move those feet!"
Now the day's over and done
Think about how much fun we had,
Curling up nice and tight
Now it's time to say goodnight!

Arissa Ali (9)
Hillside Avenue Primary And Nursery School, Norwich

A Royal's Biggest Day

It's finally the day,
Of the big celebration,
People are gathering all through the town,
I feel nervous, excited and scared to be crowned,
All different emotions are flying around,
I'm sitting on the royal throne,
Waiting and waiting, just to be crowned,
Corgis are around me like tiny bodyguards,
People are staring only at me,
I'm more nervous than I was before,
Now the Archbishop is walking down the aisle.

He's putting the crown on my head,
I'm now happy I've done it,
And I woke up in my bed and said,
"It was all fake..."

Charlotte Godfrey-Daynes (9)
Hillside Avenue Primary And Nursery School, Norwich

A Writer

A writer sits upon a hill

W ondering if the world will be still, glancing left and glancing right, he sees shooting stars

R ace through the night. He thinks of stars with great delight and says to himself

"I can see light." He closed his eyes and dreamed so bright of

T housands of fairies finally taking flight. Suddenly,

E verything's calm and everything's bright as the sun and moon dance through the night.

R apid waves shine so bright as dawn breaks, making the world alight.

Elika Rafiee (8)
Hillside Avenue Primary And Nursery School, Norwich

Flower

Into the soil, I plant a seed,
Sunlight and water, I will feed,
I'm not in a rush for it to grow,
Come rain or wind or sun or snow,
I wait and wait and soon I see,
A little bud looking up at me,
It grew and grew till the sun came down,
It makes me happy, never a frown,
The next morning, it seemed to tilt,
The flower then began to wilt,
Bye bye flower, I'll miss you so,
It's such a shame you had to go.

Keavy Taylor (9)
Hillside Avenue Primary And Nursery School, Norwich

Fairies

F abulous things fly above me,
A wonder for everyone to see.
I cannot explain how it feels,
R are creatures with wings circle me,
I start to wander staring up,
E ven though I'm getting dizzy,
S uper satisfied, I love fairies!

Zoe Asamoah (8)
Hillside Avenue Primary And Nursery School, Norwich

Monster

M any big eyes looking at me
O ver the end of my bed
N ever have I been so afraid - so I turned and fled
S omeone must be playing a trick on me
T hey took me to their lair
E verlasting stare,
R elief, it is a dream.

Sienna Fairall (9)
Hillside Avenue Primary And Nursery School, Norwich

Curiosity

One time in my dreams
I came across a door
I opened it to take a peek
And see what was in store

The sight was rather frightening
As the sky was filled with lightning
While dragons soared across the sky
My stomach started tightening

He looked fairly hungry
You could see it in his eyes
An astronaut came zooming in
And took me by surprise

Then on board his ship
I saw a jar of things
Fairies - I think they were -
With colour-changing wings

"What are those?" I asked
As I pointed to the jars
"They're cheeky little pixies
I brought them back from Mars."

He slowly released the cork
And they came flying out
I put my finger out to touch
As they began to shout

"Get away from us, you!"
As I got tickled to the ground
Why don't you have wings?
And why are you so loud?

This has been great fun
But now I have to go
I have to wake up before the alarm clock starts to blow

Wistfully I closed my eyes
And dreamt I was in bed
Then someone tapped me on the back
"It's not working!" the pixies said

I slumped into the corner
And then began to cry
The astronaut walked over
"Well, at least you tried!"

Then, suddenly, out of the blue
Came a blinding flash of light

And there I saw - the dragon!
Flying through the night

The dragon then came up to me;
"I apologise,
All that business earlier
It took me by surprise!"

Every night while I sleep
I pretend to fight
I carry a maiden on my back
And pretend to be a knight

"Can I make it up to you
And take you to your room?"
I hopped straight onto his back
And off we went - *zoom!*

Georgia Morphett (11) & Grace
Kingscourt School, Catherington

That's Strange

The world below me is wild and fair,
Things race about without a care.
But if you look closer it begins to change,
The world has become incredibly strange!
Stripy 'shrooms and giant cats,
This one is looking rather fat!

In the seas the dolphins walk,
Chattering and muttering very weird talk!
They walk around wearing caps,
Whilst their feet go flippity-flap.

High on the hills the brown bears grumble,
They grumble about their poor friend Humble.
Humble is a fish that lives in the sea,
He wears Hi Tops and loves Nike!

Tabby George (11) & Orla Charter (11)
Kingscourt School, Catherington

Losing Power

Twilight flickers,
My mind clickers,
Balls of light fill the sky,
As little twinkling fairies fly,
Across the moonlight, far away,
Time passes, night and day,
They really tried not to pout,
Because their magic had faded out...

I tried to help them, I really did,
In my mind, I wanted to bid,
All these fairies far away,
I'd wait forever and a day,

I shouldn't have worried,
I really shouldn't,
Because the next day, I got a surprise,
It really was the greatest prize...

Twilight flickers,
My mind clickers,
Balls of light fill the sky,
Across the moonlight, far away,
Time passes, night and day,

Things are definitely about to change,
Yes, life is really strange...

Cecilia Banning (11)
Kingscourt School, Catherington

A Dream

I've had a dream
A dream nowhere near to serene
The likes of it have never been seen

A dream with wild twists and turns
Strange are the lessons from which one learns

A dream so crazy it could burst from my head
It could make me dance and leap out of bed

A dream with magic and monsters alike
A dream with a narwhale riding a bike

A dream with a golden glowing light
A dream destined to last more than a night

A dream no one can really describe
That's because it's a creature in disguise.

Lara Pitcher (11)
Kingscourt School, Catherington

Nightmare!

Horses slaughtered,
Chickens chased,
Why is my mind so externally placed?

I lie in bed, my eyes twitching,
At the thought of my favourite things glitching.

Horses slaughtered,
Chickens chased,
Why is my mind so externally placed?

My body twists from side to side,
Why am I experiencing this roller coaster ride?

Horses slaughtered,
Chickens chased,
Why is my mind so externally placed?

Imogen Bartlett (10)
Kingscourt School, Catherington

My Shining Dream

In this dream, I see a world full of light,
Where love shines bright and hope takes flight.

I'm with those who elevate and inspire,
Who fuel me with passion and desire.

My dream is a place where beauty abounds,
Nature's wonders and colours astound.

I feel alive, free from all fear,
My heart overflowing with love and cheer.

As I journey on, I see miracles unveil,
And new chances prevail.

My shining dream is one of joy and grace,
Of endless blessings, and a peaceful space.

And all that happens in this dreamland,
Is hope, love and happiness firsthand.

Haroun Bassour (8)
Lark Hall Primary School, Lambeth

The Day I Flew

I was in school one day.
When I heard a bang.
I was so frightened since it was the middle of May.
I thought there was a gang
So I hid under my table
When a fairy appeared and said, "My name is Mabel.
I have come to pick up that little girl under her table."
"Ahh!" I screamed, but I went with her.
"Where are we going?" I asked her.
"Oh, I nearly forgot. I'm going to shrink you so you can
grow wings like me."
"Wow," I said.
So I flew to America, Egypt and the town

Suddenly, the sun shone brighter than ever and
Mabel started fading, I screamed
"Hush!" said Mum. "You're late for school."

Was it a dream or was it true?

Bonnie Holden (8)
Lower Darwen Primary School, Lower Darwen

Story-Tellers

Stories, stories
Some scary, others gory
Some haunt you in your sleep
Some simply make you weep
How are they created?
You'd like to know?
By story-tellers who like to show
Their talent, their power, their skill and might
But some of these stories give you a fright
All of these stories are detailed
Spun like a web
You can keep reading till it's time for bed
But there's a catch!
Some story-tellers like to hatch
Nightmares and dreams of sweets and ghosts
And some are so real it feels like
Someone's creeping up on you
But no one knows who
Story-tellers write with all they've got
Even though they might not
Feel their best
And not know the rest.

Jessica Cottam (11) & Sienna Holden (11)
Lower Darwen Primary School, Lower Darwen

The Bird

I put on my coat to get in my boat,
But on the way to my boat, I saw a goat.
Behind the goat, there was a bird,
However, the bird looked quite scared.
"What are you scared of?" I questioned the bird,
But the bird did not answer. I felt unheard.
A few moments later, the bird replied,
"I feel like I need to hide somewhere inside.
If I don't I'll be mistaken as prey
And I won't have enough time to fly away."
"Away from what? What do you mean?"
I asked, while the bird explained what it had seen.
"Away from the goat who lives near the boat,
That you like to claim as your own,
But you just let it float down at the deep dark moat."

Jessica Briggs (11)
Lower Darwen Primary School, Lower Darwen

Nightmares Came To Life

My nightmares might scare me,
But fear doesn't so I will snuggle up tight in the night
My parents kiss me and say, "Don't let the bed bugs
bite."
The nightmares go on through the night
And in the morning, I feel a pinch on my toe,
My parents say, "Monsters aren't real."
But I've got a gut feeling they're real
So when I felt that pinch on my toe,
I knew exactly what it was
I looked below and saw a little monster,
You could see the fear in my eyes
And I rushed out my room
And it was night again
I was so confused
The little monster had trapped me in my bed
So I slept and slept and I never ever woke up!

Rosie Hayes (10)
Lower Darwen Primary School, Lower Darwen

The Girl Who Gets Stuck In A Trophy

Once upon a time, a girl was playing football
She was so excited for tomorrow
For a competition
She was scared and heard a *bang, crash!*
She was scared
She ran home.
The next day she went to football,
She won the competition and was first
She was stuck in the trophy
She fell and a *bang, crash!*
Quick, she was petrified
She screamed, "Help! Help!"
When she was at the bottom
There were so many rooms
She walked in
Maybe there was...
No, she could not!
She tried every door
She was stuck in it...

Gracie Wilson (9)
Lower Darwen Primary School, Lower Darwen

Nightmares

N othing had prepared me for the challenges ahead
I take a look, it's full of zombies, they're trying to scare me
G lancing left and right they've all got no heads,
H ow did this happen? What in the world? I hope it's just a joke
T *hud!* Something moves, everything is creepy
M y worst fear is here, right in front of my eyes
A rock starts to rumble, oh no
R eally, really greasy
E verywhere the skies are grey
S lowly, slowly I wake up and realise it's all a nightmare.

Aizah Qureshi (9)
Lower Darwen Primary School, Lower Darwen

Free Palestine

From the river to the sea
Palestine will be free.
Please just save these children's lives
And if you do, you will get lots of high fives.

From the river to the sea
Palestine must be freed.
In Palestine there's not much food in sight
So if you help them you will see the light.

Free Palestine! Free Palestine!

From the river to the sea
Palestine will be free.
There are no wizards that can do the job
So let's save Palestine before their land gets robbed.

Free Palestine! Free Palestine!

Adam Patel (10)
Lower Darwen Primary School, Lower Darwen

Royalty

Where am I? Where could I be? What is this gorgeous land I see?
I see a castle, surrounded by knights
Confused and scared, I curl up in a fright
And then someone asked me, "My Queen, are you alright?"
I looked up at him and said, "What do you mean?"
He replied, "You are the Queen!"
I wonder in shock
Is this my castle?
Are these my knights?
Is this my kingdom?
Wow, it's all mine!
As soon as I went into the castle,
Beautiful and bold,
I woke up in my bedroom,
Tired and cold.

Elza Bachare (10)
Lower Darwen Primary School, Lower Darwen

The Lost Boy And The Sloth

The boy was lost
And
Scared
He thought he
Was
Stuck
He tried and tried
But
He
Could not
Get out of the
Rainforest
When a unicorn came
The unicorn said,
"No, no, no!"
Then monkeys
Then elephants
And a sloth.

Austin Davis (9)
Lower Darwen Primary School, Lower Darwen

The Wicked Witch

"Ha, ha, ha,"
Goes the ugly, green witch,

Purr, purr, purr,
Goes the unlucky, black cat.

Creak, creak, creak,
Goes the witch
On the stairs.

Scratch, scratch, scratch,
Goes the wolf
In the woods.

Olivia Rogers (8)
Lower Darwen Primary School, Lower Darwen

The Top Hat

T he fancy dancy hat
H armful magic
E xtraordinary

T he hat with a mind of its own
O nly worn by royalty
P oem reader

H ave I got this?
A nd if I haven't, I need it
T roublemaker.

Katie Nightingale (9)
Lower Darwen Primary School, Lower Darwen

Tommy's Run

Tommy goes left
Tommy goes right
Tommy goes straight
Into a fright
Tommy goes "Wee!"
Tommy goes *thud*
Tommy goes *bang! Bang! Bang! Bang!*
Tommy stands up
Tommy falls down
Then he ripped his gown.
Tommy had a frown.

Logan Lewis (10), Theodore Orrell (10) & William Murphy (10)
Lower Darwen Primary School, Lower Darwen

The Night I Got Stuck In Candy Land

C reature gummies
A chocolate river
N othing better
D rizzling marshmallows
Y ummy, yummy.

L ollipops
A nd jelly babies
N ever healthy
D elicious candy.

Esta Mason-Tabbinor (8)
Lower Darwen Primary School, Lower Darwen

The Fat Cat In A Hat On A Mat

I had a cat
Who was so fat.
He could not even
Sit on his mat.
He had a hat
That did not fit.
He put it on
And then it split!

Alfie Montague (10)
Lower Darwen Primary School, Lower Darwen

The Cat

There once was a cat
Who lived in a hat
Which jumped at a rat
And hid under a mat
And their name is Pat and they go
Ratatat.

Freya Eccles (10)
Lower Darwen Primary School, Lower Darwen

My Dreamland

So last night I fell asleep
The next morning I was in my
Dreamland
I went outside
And I saw unicorns and sloths.

Phoebe Hibbert (8)
Lower Darwen Primary School, Lower Darwen

Nightmares!

N ightmares are terrifying just like this one,

I step into a world of horror with my brothers,

G lancing left and right, I see a clown with dead spiders,

H ow awful it is!

T hunder strikes behind us,

M y brother defends himself against the clown and he runs away,

A re you scared of nightmares like me?

R oyalty has them, even they cannot be spared,

E veryone has them, how often do you?

S uddenly, I wake up and I'm glad it's just a dream but you might wake up with a loud scream!

Monica Ruggieri (8)
Moor End Community Primary School, Oswaldtwistle

My Clown Nightmare

N othing has prepared me for this scary moment,

I see a scary monster in the corner of my eye,

G etting scared, I look to my right, "Oh no, I see another!

H elp me, someone!

T his is scary," I scream.

M y eyes start tearing up, there's nothing I can do

A nd suddenly, more clowns appear

R unning around everywhere

E verything I look at goes blurry, I can't take this anymore,

S uddenly, I scream, then wake up and find I'm safe at home.

Harper Taylor (9)
Moor End Community Primary School, Oswaldtwistle

Nightmares

N ighttime is when monsters do crimes

I nside your closet will be a trap

G oing outside will be a big mistake...

H ave to run away to somewhere safe.

T omorrow, monsters wait for the dark sky to come

M ysterious devil faces under your bed.

A spider dropping from your light.

R emember your other dreams rotting in the past

E veryone has nightmares so don't feel scared!

S uddenly I wake up and I'm safe in my bed.

Elsa Taylor (9)
Moor End Community Primary School, Oswaldtwistle

Nightmares

N auseous and terrified, I appear in an abandoned shop,
I see a clown laughing at me,
G azing and gulping at the clown I take a step back
H aunted with horror, I freeze with fright,
T he lights flicker and turn off!
M aybe this is the worst day of my life,
A nd it's even more creepy now,
R umours say clowns kill,
E nding is for me, I wish to be free
S and falls from the ceiling and I get buried.

Catelyn O'Rourke (9)
Moor End Community Primary School, Oswaldtwistle

The Nightmares I Always Had

N obody loves nightmares, they hate them
I n bed but you're having nightmares
G lancing at your room all night, then wake up screaming
H aving nightmares and you're terrified
T rying to get rid of your nightmares
M y mind is full of scary things
A hh! People are screaming
R unning away but the creepy monsters are following you
E ars are ringing from petrified cries
S top the monsters!

Lachlan Mclennan (8)
Moor End Community Primary School, Oswaldtwistle

Untitled

N oise is coming out of nowhere
I could not tell what was going on
G uy someone was shouting, "Guy!"
H e was very strange and looked like a black figure
T he black figure looked a bit creepy
M e, I felt very scared and anxious
A nd I could not risk myself getting killed
R ight now it was time to go and run.
E very step I took it felt like the figure was getting closer.

Sarim Ali Hashmi (9)
Moor End Community Primary School, Oswaldtwistle

Nightmares

N ightmares are the worst
I 've got the worst anybody can have
G loomy night we went to the play centre
H ow's it weird?
T *ick, tock* goes the clock
"M are," I hear clowns say, but without the night
A little clown voice creeps up to me
"R oar!" said a clown with a toy dinosaur
"E at you!" and then suddenly, I woke up.

Oscar Speight (8)
Moor End Community Primary School, Oswaldtwistle

Candyland

C andy, everywhere you look,

A n enormous amount of it,

N ever will you ever run out,

D elicious candy you didn't think was real,

Y ou're with your friend Elsa and a unicorn,

L ounging about in your PJs,

A nimals are very playful in this land, you see,

N ever will you want to leave,

D evils and monsters are banned from this beautiful place.

Skylar Shaw (9)
Moor End Community Primary School, Oswaldtwistle

Clown's Fair

N ightmares are scary like this one,
I t was dark at the fair
G lancing into the clown's fair
H ow did it get here?
T *hud!* There was a scary clown,
M y fear is standing in front of me!
A creepy smile appears on the clown's face
R unning as fast as I can...
E ars are hearing things...
S uddenly I woke up screaming!

Eric Allen (8)
Moor End Community Primary School, Oswaldtwistle

Creepy-Crawley Spiders

S pooky spiders at night coming into your home.
P eople scream and shout when they see them!
I n the night they make their home.
D o they explore around your home when you don't know?
E scaping them is tricky
R un away if you can.
S pend the night away from them and dream a happy dream if you can.

Ruby Clarke (8)
Moor End Community Primary School, Oswaldtwistle

My Animal Adventure

A field full of animals,

N ewborn pups led by their mums,

I nside or outside fluffy animals everywhere,

M any cows eating the grass,

A nd the horses galloping around,

L ambing season had arrived,

S oon my eyes start to open and... I'm awake from my dream.

Alaena Whyte (9)
Moor End Community Primary School, Oswaldtwistle

My Teaching Life

I dream of being a teacher
I hope to pass on my skills
I hope they listen well

I dream of being a teacher
I hope my children are respectful
I hope they enjoy school

I dream of being a teacher
I hope I am teaching at an excellent school
I hope I get the job.

Sophie Beeston (9)
Moor End Community Primary School, Oswaldtwistle

Clowns

C lowns making scary faces
L et's not let the zombies suck out our brains
O w, that hurt
W hat was it...?
N ot a clown, not a zombie, it was a...!
S uddenly, I woke up safe in bed.

Asa Solch (9)
Moor End Community Primary School, Oswaldtwistle

Rathi

R oasting hot volcanos nearby
A scorched land of nothingness
T errifyingly long wings
H orrifyingly sharp teeth
I nstant destruction everywhere.

Cody Long (9)
Moor End Community Primary School, Oswaldtwistle

My Cat

I am lost in the woods, nothing to see
Apart from my cat who is 103
I walk up to a door on the side of a tree
I appear on a running track and a pirate is chasing me.

I hide under a hurdle, I run a lap of the track
All to get away from a pirate attack
Then I realise that it's not a pirate but a monster in
disguise, that's chasing me around whilst double my
size.

Then my cat grew and grew until it was huge.
As big as an elephant that escaped from the zoo
Next, it turned black, then grew four extra legs
It turned into a spider with curly hair
Then scared the monster back into its lair
My cat turned back from a scary old fright
To my cute little cat, snuggled up for the night.

Ollie Attah (9)
Newbridge Primary School, Bath

Nightmare

In the dark land, I can see,
A cave as jagged as can be.
Rocks like daggers piercing out,
One wrong move and it'll be blackout.
Suddenly I hear a scream,
It sounds like death, I hope it's a dream.
Then I hear another after,
Followed by wicked laughter.
All of a sudden out comes a mean
Killer clown that I have seen.
It takes out a knife covered in blood,
And says to me, "You're next bud."
It starts to chase me, I think I'm dead,
I hope I wake up in bed.
Then another comes along,
To join in with the other one.
As I run I trip on a lump of lead,
But I find myself safe in bed.

Jake Snook (10)
Newbridge Primary School, Bath

Dreamland

I glimpsed an eye of a twinkling light,
Above my head a starry night,
Down lay my dog in the fog,
Above grew baby trees,
Up to my knees,
A chocolate floor,
And a doomy door,
So I went in,
With a scared-looking grin,
Below me, I saw branches scattered all over the floor,
I looked up and saw,
A great big dinosaur,
So I ran and I ran,
But the door has now slammed,
I am now out of breath,
But I cannot rest,
But then I woke,
And now I cannot speak,
I am now scared,
So I go downstairs,
To go to my mum,
And tell her I did not have fun.

Cerys Little (10)
Newbridge Primary School, Bath

Every Night

In my bed every night,
A dream I might have might give me a fright,
Or hiccups or headlice, you roll the dice,
I close my eyes and count to ten.
Sometimes, I see a giant hen,
My imagination dances
At all the different chances,
I could be a nurse
In a different universe,
A gnome
Who lives in a dome,
A cook
Reading a book,
But most of all, I could be
Anything that was my cup of tea,
And when I wake up the next day,
It will all start again for me to play.

Isla Stacey (10)
Newbridge Primary School, Bath

Darkness

I can see darkness all around,
There is nothing to be seen but a distant sound.
Perhaps I was in a dream,
But no, I was nowhere to be seen.
"What must I do?" I cried and screamed,
But still, there was nothing to be seen.
I hid under my covers, not knowing what to do,
Suddenly, I heard a big bang!
It was coming up the stairs,
My door creaked open like a squeak of a mouse!
In a blink of an eye, I noticed
It was all just a dream.

Elsa Wicks (10)
Newbridge Primary School, Bath

Fearless

F ear is not an option in this mythical land
E ven though there is a band of evil lambs
A s you run you lose your way
R unning even faster, you turn the wrong way
L osing hope, you turn back in dismay
E leven lambs are coming your way
S crambling and falling down a hill
S oon, you will outrun this evil band of lambs.

Because you should
Never give up.

Isobel Manners (10)
Newbridge Primary School, Bath

Return To Dasedron Island

D ry wastelands
A nd
S uper swamps
E xotic creatures
D ragons, dinos and rarely monsters
R oaring giants
O x overlords
N ight is day, day is night

I n the dark, light shall rise
S ky will fall if not for the four...
L agon egg
A ncro egg
N anano egg
D ragon egg.

Eli Robertson (9)
Newbridge Primary School, Bath

Fearless

F ear is not an option in this mythical land
E ven though there is a band of evil lambs
A s you run, you lose your way
R unning even faster you turn the wrong way
L osing hope, you turn back in dismay
E leven lambs are coming your way
S crambling and falling down a hill
S oon you will outrun this evil bunch of lambs.

Henry Navias (9)
Newbridge Primary School, Bath

I Rise

You may shove, tease, hit and hurt me,
With your hurtful pushes and your hurtful lies,
You destroy my heart with sadness and angriness,
You may push me down into the dark dirt,
But still, like an angel floating in the sky.
I rise.
Just like a new day when you wake up you smile,
With the courage of a rainbow brightening up the sky
with lovely colours,
Just like wishes flying up high in the sky,
Still, I rise.
Did you know your lies want me to cry until I drown in
the water,
Like the salt sea water in the yellow sand?
But still, I rise.
On the surface floating, swimming from deep and high
water,
I rise.
Leaping up, crashing, thrashing like waves,
I rise.
I'm a stallion, roaring in the tide,
I am a tree in a storm, my strength belied,
I rise.

Saying goodbye to days of pain and fear,
I rise.
Entering into a world that blossoms around me.
I rise.
From the love and support of those around me,
Now I can see the light.
I am the dream, the hope, and have the power to fight through.
I rise, I rise, I rise.

Mia Gowling (8)
Nicholas Hawksmoor Primary School, Towcester

I Rise

You may discriminate me, eliminate me,
With your mocking laughs, slanderous cries,
Your rolling eyes.

You may push me down in the city sewers,
But like a rocket flying to space, I rise.

Just like the tides coming in and out,
And the stars which sit in space twinkling,
The planets, the moons never stop spinning,
Like goals aiming beyond the sky,
I rise.

Do you want to see me crumble, sinking to my knees?
Do you want to see me shattered into a thousand
pieces?
Do you want to see me crumble like a tower of Lego
bricks falling to the ground?
Teardrops falling from the sky gloomily,
Broken by my cries.

On the surface, still standing, charging,
Resisting, nothing can stop me, like the Earth's
atmosphere,
I am a tsunami, crashing wide,

I am a tiger roaring with pride.
I will not give up.

Fleeing the years of fright and sadness,
I rise.
Embracing a new world where the blossoms surround me,
Making adventures,
I rise.

From the depths of despair to the highs of life,
I rise.
But I am the future, the confidence building inside me.
I rise, I rise, I rise.

Seiki Komatsu (9)
Nicholas Hawksmoor Primary School, Towcester

Rainbow

Dreams are
A rainbow cloud burst
A lovely sound softly heard
A rainbow cloud burst
A best rain slowly falling
A colourful picture of family
Clear and surprisingly good.

Nightmares are
A scary black and white cloud
A bad sound loudly heard
A scary black and white cloud
A worrying rain quickly falling
A grey picture of bees
Restless and surprisingly bad.

Max Drew (8)
Okehampton Primary School And Foundation Unit, Okehampton

The Alphabet Dream

A rranging dream lots

B eing beautiful

D ream giver

E ggs, elephants and elegance

F ell in a dream

G oing into Dreamland

H orrifying nightmares

I scream

J ack-o'-lanterns

K iller cats

L ightning dreams

M uttering mustard

N ature

O ceans

P oles

Q ueens and Kings

R hyming words

S ongs and singing

T ea and honey

U mbrellas, floating in the sky

V eils and shadows

W aves in the sea

X oxo

Y ou're my sunshine
Z uzanna's and Lena's dreams.

Zuzanna Krzysiek (7)
Okehampton Primary School And Foundation Unit, Okehampton

Spot

My mum bought me a puppy
And I have called him Spot
I cuddle him and brush him
And play with him a lot
I take him out on nice long walks
And watch him jump and run
While I teach him to fetch the ball
And we both have loads of fun
But best of all, when I'm tired
And asleep on the settee
My best friend Spot will be on my lap
And snoring just like me.

Kensi Pettis (8)
Okehampton Primary School And Foundation Unit, Okehampton

In My Magical Dreams

I'd rather be magic than not
I'd rather be cold than hot
I'd rather be a fairy than a witch
I'd rather be flying that in a ditch
I'd rather be a little child than a giant
I'd rather be good than defiant
I'd rather be an alien than a girl
I'd rather be able to stretch than twirl
Make my magical dreams come true.

Hetty Stevens (7)
Okehampton Primary School And Foundation Unit, Okehampton

Unicorn

A big, sharp horn
Four pretty hooves
A rainbow tail

Eat colourful apples
Long, flying wings
Galloping in the galaxy
Walking on the rainbow
They spit out her mouth

The unicorn is fighting with humans.

Paige Baily (7)
Okehampton Primary School And Foundation Unit, Okehampton

Family

We go to Legoland to smile
And have fun
But most of all we have fun
The most important thing is we play
We are kind
We all share.

Lyla Gibbs (8)
Okehampton Primary School And Foundation Unit, Okehampton

A Nightmare School

It's hard starting a new school,
New looks,
New clothes,
New shoes.
You get the partner, you do not choose,
And they give you answer clues,
Which is completely not true
Now I have this gloom in my mood,
This is stopping the way I feel good
All I want is to go to bed,
Wishing this to get out of my head
Now I feel cold shivers down my spine,
This is such a terrible crime.

Fareeha Memon (8)
Ormiston Meadows Academy, Peterborough

What Is My Dream?

Is it?

Flying in the sky like a bird,
Or talking to a science nerd,
But, what is my dream?

Is it?

Joining a pirate's clan,
Even meeting Superman,
But, what is my dream?

Is it?

Getting lost in a dark cave,
Or meeting a spider called Dave,
But, what is my dream?

Evelyn Geary (8)
Outwood Primary Academy Kirkhamgate, Kirkhamgate

My Dreams

M y dreams will come true
Y our dreams may come true

D reams will always be there
R eading is fun
E ager to be a footballer
A lways be happy with dreams
M ake more dreams, more dreams are better
S o be happy with your dreams!

Harry Robinson (8)
Outwood Primary Academy Kirkhamgate, Kirkhamgate

Sound Collector

Inspired by 'The Sound Collector' by Roger McGough

A fairy called last night,
Dressed all in rainbow and grey,
Put every sound into a purse,
And carried them away.

The barking of the dog,
The flap of the wings,
The sound of the wind,
The rattling of the rings.

The stomping of the gig,
The scratching of the cat,
The clucking of the hen,
The attacking of the rat.

The splashing of the pool,
The banging of the tool,
The oinking of the pig,
The sound of the pitch.

A fairy called last night,
She didn't leave her name,
Left us only silence,
Life will never be the same!

Leila-May Lugg (7)
Ribbon Academy, Murton

Sound Collector

Inspired by 'The Sound Collector' by Roger McGough

A dragon called this afternoon,
Dressed all in red and grey,
Put every sound into a cup,
And pushed them away.

The honking of the pig,
The scraping of the louse,
The itching of the wig,
The squeaking of the mouse.

The swishing of the bat,
The cracking of the dish,
The quacking of the duck,
The splashing of the fish.

The scratching of the mouse,
The chirping of the wren,
The rolling of the log,
The flapping of the hen.

The laughing of the baby,
The rallying of the bear,
The honking of the car,
The jumping of the hare.

The trumping of the elephant,
The croaking of the frog,
The dropping of the hat,
The barking of the dog.

A dragon called this afternoon,
She didn't leave her name,
Left us only silence,
Life will never be the same!

Cora Smith (8)
Ribbon Academy, Murton

Sound Collector

Inspired by 'The Sound Collector' by Roger McGough

A demon called last night
Dressed all in black and grey
Put every sound into a sack
And sneaked them away.

The knocking of the door
The swishing of the trees
The crunching of the bun
The buzzing of the bees.

The barking of the dog
The smashing of the glass
The splashing of the wave
The shouting of the class.

The crying of the baby
The reading of the stairs
The sizzling of the pan
The juicing of the pear.

The shutting of the door
The squeaking of the rat
The dripping of the tap
The meowing of the cat.

The snoring of the dad
The turning of the jar
The spinning of the roundabout
The stomping of the bar.

A demon called last night
She didn't leave her name
Left us only silence
Life will never be the same!

Gracie Purvis (8)
Ribbon Academy, Murton

Sound Collector

Inspired by 'The Sound Collector' by Roger McGough

A demon called this evening,
Dressed all in red and grey,
Put every sound into a sack
And took them away.

The sizzling of the bacon
The shining of the sun
The splashing of the pool
The crunching of the bun.

The crunching of the ice cream cone
The splashing of the pool
The blowing of the fan
The squeaking of the rat

The sizzling of the fire
The meowing of the cat
The screwing of the nail
The squeaking of the rat

The crying of the baby
The meowing of the cat
The squealing of the pig
The smashing of the gate

The swishing of the bird
The swooshing of the pen
The whack of the ball
The tweeting of the wren

A demon called this evening
She didn't leave her name,
Left us only silence,
Life will never be the same!

Victoria Ann Byles (8)
Ribbon Academy, Murton

Sound Collector

Inspired by 'The Sound Collector' by Roger McGough

A football player called this morning
Dressed all in gold and grey
Put every sound into a wallet
And took them away

The crunching of the ice cream
The swishing of the football
The bang of the goal
The bash of the sports hall

The squirting of the sun cream
The woof of the dog
The swirl of the football
The honking of the hog

The squish of the squashy
The swirling of the run
The swarf of the ball
The bash of the goal

The sizzling of the barbecue
The scratching of the cat
The crunch of the ice cream
The *ratatating* of the rat

Once Upon A Dream - Whispers Of Dreams

A footballer called this morning
He didn't leave his name
Left us only silence
Life will never be the same!

Freddie Pinder (8)
Ribbon Academy, Murton

Sound Collector

Inspired by 'The Sound Collector' by Roger McGough

A football player called this morning
Dressed all in red and grey,
Put every sound into a pack
And kicked them away.

The splashing of the water
The flapping of the bird
The slithering of the snake
The silence of the word

The bashing of the ball
The hitting of the rat
The flapping of the bird
The bashing of the cat

The sizzling of the BBQ
The oinking of the pig
The spraying of the cream
The watching of the wig

The smiling of the child
The scraping of the pin
The munching of the bun
The swimming of the dolphin

A football player called this morning
He didn't leave his name,
He only left us silence,
Life will never be the same!

Theo Fawcett (8)
Ribbon Academy, Murton

Sound Collector

Inspired by 'The Sound Collector' by Roger McGough

A fairy called this morning,
Dressed all in white and grey,
Put every sound in a big bag,
And carried them away.

The ticking of the clock,
The oinking of the pig,
The bursting of the drain,
The swishing of a wig.

The splashing of the fish,
The meowing of the cat,
The smashing of the dish,
The crunching of the hat.

The beeping of the train,
The barking of the dog,
The tapping of the rain,
The swishing of the bog.

The roaring of the bear,
The moaning of the boy,
The laughing of the children,
The clicking of the toy.

A fairy called this morning,
And didn't leave her name,
Left us only silence,
Life will never be the same!

Ava Florence Emmerson (7)
Ribbon Academy, Murton

Sound Collector

Inspired by 'The Sound Collector' by Roger McGough

A wizard called yesterday,
Dressed all in blue and grey,
Put every sound into a teapot
And poofed them away.

The barking of the dog,
The laughing of the boy,
The splashing of the fish,
The squeaking of the toy.

The smashing of the dishes,
The roaring of the bear,
The squealing of the bat,
The stomping of the boot.

The tweeting of the wren,
The cracking of the log,
The beeping of the cars,
The ribbiting of the frog.

The sucking of the drain,
The purring of the cat,
The squeaking of the mouse,
The dropping of the hat.

A wizard called yesterday
He didn't leave his name,
Left us only silence,
Life will never be the same!

Robert Charlton (8)
Ribbon Academy, Murton

Sound Collector

Inspired by 'The Sound Collector' by Roger McGough

A lady called this morning,
Dressed all in yellow and grey,
Put every sound into a pot,
And put them away.

The crashing of the glass,
The banging of the bat,
The closing of the book,
The sliding of the mat.

The honking of the cars,
The barking of the dog,
The smashing of the dish,
The rolling of the log.

The ticking of the clock,
The choo-ing of the train,
The oinking of the pig,
The gurgling of the drain.

The dropping of the hat,
The chatting of the girl,
The squishing of the squishy,
The cracking of the pearl.

A lady called this morning.
She didn't leave her name,
Left us only silence,
Life will never be the same.

Kai Johnson (8)
Ribbon Academy, Murton

Sound Collector

Inspired by 'The Sound Collector' by Roger McGough

A demon called this morning
Dressed all in red and grey,
Put every sound into a skull
And took them away.

The hissing of the kitten
The smashing of the glass
The banging of the game
The scariness of the class

The tweeting of the wren
The splashing of the pool
The creaking of the stairs
The nonsense of the fool

The yumminess of the ice cream
The writing of the pen
The fun of the Barbie
The playing of the Ken

The crying of the baby
The noise of the pig
The losing of the tablet
The flapping of the wig

A demon called this morning
She didn't leave her name,
Left us only silence,
Life will never be the same!

Courtney Wilkinson (8)
Ribbon Academy, Murton

Sound Collector

Inspired by 'The Sound Collector by Roger McGough

A man called this morning,
Dressed in black and grey,
Put every sound into a box,
And took them away.

The swishing of the water,
The playing of the boy,
The barking of the dog,
The scratching of the toy.

The banging of the hammer,
The running of the dog,
The ticking of the clock,
The rolling of the log.

The flying of the birds,
The oinking of the pig,
The banging of the head,
The swishing of the wig.

The ticking of the time,
The meowing of the cat,
The banging of the door,
The falling of the hat

A man called today,
He didn't leave his name,
Left us only silence,
Life will never be the same!

Caiden Adams (8)
Ribbon Academy, Murton

Sound Collector

Inspired by 'The Sound Collector' by Roger McGough

A wizard called this dinnertime,
Dressed all in blue and grey,
Put every sound into a bag
And careered them away.

The swish of the wand
The smell of the smoke
The dazzle of the magic
The swoosh of the cloak.

The bang of the fire
The power of the spell
The heat of the power
The bang of the well.

The smell of the house
The bang of the pool
The bang of the wand
The bang of the floor.

A wizard called this dinnertime
He didn't leave his name
Left us only silence
Life will never be the same!

Lynkon Spooner (7)
Ribbon Academy, Murton

Sound Collector

Inspired by 'The Sound Collector' by Roger McGough

A dragon called this afternoon,
Dressed all in red and grey,
Put every sound into a pot,
And threw them away.

The roaring of the lion,
The barking of the dogs,
The trumpeting of the elephant,
The croaking of the frog.

The chatting of the people,
The flapping of the fish,
The beeping of cars,
The crashing of the dish.

A dragon called this afternoon,
He didn't leave his name,
Left us only silence,
Life will never be the same!

Jacobjohn Self (7), Christopher & Great
Ribbon Academy, Murton

Sound Collector

Inspired by 'The Sound Collector' by Roger McGough

A witch called this evening
Dressed all in blue and grey
Put every sound into a safe
And locked them away.

The sizzling of the barbecue
The snoring of the cat
The swishing of the wind
The clucking of the hat.

The stomping of the giant
The smell of the smoke
The mess of the bed
The laughing of the joke.

A witch called this evening
She didn't leave her name
Left us only silence
Life will never be the same!

Harper
Ribbon Academy, Murton

Sound Collector

Inspired by 'The Sound Collector' by Roger McGough

A fairy called yesterday,
Dressed all in blue and grey,
Put every sound into a lid,
And took them away.

The bubbling of the drain,
The meow of the cat,
The woof of the dog,
The crunch of the mat.

The scream of the boy,
The cluck of the hen,
The splashing of the fish,
The scratch of the pen.

A fairy called yesterday,
But didn't leave his name,
Left us only silence,
Life will never be the same!

Wyatt Ball (7)
Ribbon Academy, Murton

Sound Collector

Inspired by 'The Sound Collector' by Roger McGough

A dragon called this afternoon,
Dressed all in red and grey,
Put every sound into a pot,
And threw them away.

The roaring of the lion,
The barking of the dog,
The trumpeting of the elephant,
The crunching of the log.

A dragon called this afternoon,
He didn't leave his name,
Left us only silence,
Life will never be the same!

Lucy Newton (7)
Ribbon Academy, Murton

Sound Collector

Inspired by 'The Sound Collector' by Roger McGough

A zombie called last night,
Dressed all in blue and grey,
Put every sound into a brain,
And carried them away.

The smell of the smoke,
The scratching of the wall,
The crunching of the crisps,
The echo of the hall.

A zombie called last night,
He didn't leave his name,
Left us only silence,
Life will never be the same!

Zak
Ribbon Academy, Murton

The Best Holiday

A nice day, a very nice day today, I am
In the pool and it feels very, very nice
And I got an ice cream
I have the best holiday in the world
Just one more thing I need is
My friends
Lilly, Rose, Millie and Chloe
A nice day, a very nice day today
I am in the pool and
I got an ice cream
And the pool feels
Very, very nice
I got a lemon ice cream
I love it, I love it
It is the best holiday
I love it, I love it
I just need one more thing which is
My friends.

Darcey Corbett (7)
Seend CE Primary School, Seend

Fairy Dust

I close my eyes and relax,
I find that there are fairies everywhere,
Some are here, and some are here, and some are there,
And some are putting flowers in my hair,
They had sugar plums and daisy shows,
They also sing me lullabies.
I take a walk with the Fairy Queen,
Then I lie down in a pile of soft roses,
I feel happy and tired,
I wave goodbye to the fairies and dragons and unicorns,
Then I woke up in the woods on my picnic blanket!

Rose Freegard (8)
Seend CE Primary School, Seend

Fairies

F airies are everywhere and I should know because I am

A fairy, you might be wondering who

I am. I am crazy but I am

R ight. You might also be wondering what powers I have. Like

I don't know everything but I am the fairy of

E arth. Oh, and if you are reading this in 5000 years time, then

S top.

Chloe Grabham (7)
Seend CE Primary School, Seend

Unicorn

U no day I saw,
N o dark, but I did see light,
I could see unicorns and fairies,
C ircling around me and
O n top of the biggest cloud a,
R ough chair was there and they said that,
N o one had seen this. Just then I woke up.

Faye Long (8)
Seend CE Primary School, Seend

Mooshmallow Land

M y dream starts with Nia, a fairy
O f Mooshmallow Land
O n a cotton candy cloud
S uperpowers Nia has to make unicorns
H owever, afraid of dragons she is
M ooshmallow
A land of floaty fairy dancers
L oving and delightful
L avender mist and
O range blossom scents wafted through the air
W himsical land of Mooshmallow!

Nuha Jasrul Azily (9)
St Bride's Primary School, Belfast

The Cat On The Road: A Really Weird Poem

The cat on the road
On the road, he drove
And didn't know what was next
He passed away and laid his head
On the hay right down his back
They made a potion and poured it on a cushion
And saw the cat all shivering
They saw him alive and gave a sigh.

Evelina Khaidanova (8)
St Bride's Primary School, Belfast

School Nightmare

Once upon a dream, the school will dread;
This horrid name, 'school', is just another name for prison.

All the schools around the world
Hate liberty and freedom for the school system is unjust and unfair.

School was good and fair when Miss Gilligan was teaching Year 6
But when Sir took over, we were on our knees.

Then World War III began
Kids vs teachers
The teachers lost but at a great cost
Most kids were hurt or worse.

Sir has been fired now
And we all wake up to the sweet song of birds
Or so we thought
It turns out the dream became real
Most of my friends are hurt, some are gone
Those who survived live in a secret location

We are plotting our revenge on the outside world
We have the right...

All we know is we will do it at night
And attack on kites.

All things on Earth will rejoice from the song
Of the children's choir
For kids will destroy the school and remake it in their
image
School will be fun and nice and all people like Sir will be
in detention forever
Best of all
Miss Gilligan will teach Year 6.

Theo Mason-Diamond (10)
St Christopher's RC Primary School, Ashton-Under-Lyne

The Mystical Dream That I Could Only Have

In my mystical dream,
I think of the places where I have been,
Then I start the real supreme deal.

I ride on a shooting star,
And I shoot with glee as I go afar.
I know I'm loud but I'm
Surely proud that I'm taking a
Step this far.

In my mystical dream,
I land on the moon
But I'm sure I'll have fun anytime soon.
I explore the land and I clearly
Demand, I can't have fun all alone.

I explore some more, check every inch,
But I feel like I'm not alone,
That's for sure!

I turn around and suddenly
See a friendly creature
In front of me.

I lead her to my sparkling
Ride and she says I'm a
Superstar!

Finally say goodbye to
My friend, I determinedly ride
Back home, have some tea
And cuddle my teddy - Mr Gnome!

I wake up in the morning
And think this was the best
Dream I've ever had and I
Just wish my real life won't
Be too sad.

Sofia Gabrane (11)
St Christopher's RC Primary School, Ashton-Under-Lyne

A Dream To Remember

In the deep, deep dark,
When silence is sullen,
And the quiet is deafening,
A spark erupts,
It expands and grows stronger, and stronger,
The black canvas is filled with vibrance and vastness,
Fine works of imagination burst into light.

In my dreams, the sky was blue,
The sun was warm and the grass was green,
And in the distance, I saw a rainbow span,
A kaleidoscope of colour, like nothing else I'd seen.

The trees were bright with falling foliage,
The river flowed with shining light,
And as I ventured deeper, I found the top of a
mountain, high,
And I bathed in the colours of the sky,
With the sun, the wind, the stars and the moon by my
side.

It was a dream that felt so real,
So full of colour and beauty,
And when I woke, I couldn't help but smile,

Knowing that such a dream was meant for me to see,
And that one day, I might be able to make it a reality.

Jessica Thompson (11)
St Christopher's RC Primary School, Ashton-Under-Lyne

Hedgehog And Porcupine

H e is fluffy and blue and gives me joy
E ven when I'm sad, he is my favourite toy!
D uring the night, he grew into a giant
G rinning down at me like I were an ant
E xcited to play with my huge, spiky friend
H im and I realised good things can come to an end
O n a comfy chair, he gave me a smiley beam
G etting out of bed, I realise it was a dream

P erhaps we should get some company
O ne porcupine for him and me
R eady for our friend, we extend the toy house
C oming inside, he sees a mouse
U h oh, something isn't right
P orcupine turned the day to night?
I n confusion, I go to bed,
N ot doing anything, I lay my head
E ven after this, it was just a dream.

Elise Foronda (10)
St Christopher's RC Primary School, Ashton-Under-Lyne

The Penguin And The Goose

This is a penguin and a goose,
They are friends, they share a shed,
They play a game and when they play a game,
They always go to a shed.

The goose and the penguin will always eat food,
Like fish and chips with a piece of bread,
And when the penguin says, "What's inside the bread?"
The goose says, "There's always wheat."

The goose and the penguin will always play,
Go to an ice fortress or a pond,
If they go to the pond, they always fall,
The ice fortress is very slippery,
If they go, they will become a piece of paper.

The penguins and the goose will go to bed,
If they don't go to sleep,
They will get bitten by bed bugs and go to sleep,
The penguin and goose are in a dream,
Where the poem goes to sleep.

Tadek Chmara (10)
St Christopher's RC Primary School, Ashton-Under-Lyne

A Surprising Dream

In a cosy bed, I laid my head,
Drifting off as I went to bed.
A dream filled my sleepy mind,
Taking me to a world I'd never find.
Driving the car, with the sun so bright,
Through the day and into the night.
Our car in the air, oh what a terrible sight,
Floating high on a breeze so light.
With my friend beside me, filled with fear,
We cried out in panic, shedding a tear,
To the navy blue sky, we were led,
Where the moon awaited, so cold, so dread.
Reaching for the stars, we ventured far,
Glimpsing Mars, shining like a distant star.
Amongst it all, a mystical creature appeared,
Its wonders and secrets, we eagerly neared.
Unfortunately, I woke up.

Aleesha Abraham (11)
St Christopher's RC Primary School, Ashton-Under-Lyne

My Fantasy World

In my dream world, I'm bouncing on clouds,
And I am screaming out loud.
Golden yellow sunflowers surround me,
And colourful rainbows float above me.
Nature paints the sky blue,
And I have to say this isn't new.
Trees sway and dance,
And bushes prance.
I'm leaping across the verdant fields,
And I'm jumping over crumpled leaves.
I feel exuberant in the world,
And I don't want it to stop.
But then I woke up,
And realised that I was in a dream.

Nevil Jishore Thuruthen (10)
St Christopher's RC Primary School, Ashton-Under-Lyne

Rainbow Girl Had A Dream

I prance like unicorns dancing on rainbows
I feel so happy while my mind makes tornadoes

I am getting lost
In the world of Jack Frost

Flying like fairies
Near a fountain

Dragons are wizards that ride the stars
And play their guitars

Monsters are cars
That fly to Mars

Writers can dream
Because they make the scene.

Layla Boardman (11)
St Christopher's RC Primary School, Ashton-Under-Lyne

The Fashion Dream

In my dreams every night
I see myself in the light
My future seems so bright
Even though it might not work out.

Tonight is a delight
Besides I need to decide
If I can pursue my dreams
To be a fashion queen
So I need to have passion
About the pattern
I use for the fabric
So I can be fantastic.

Harper Thompstone (10)
St Christopher's RC Primary School, Ashton-Under-Lyne

An Astronaut's Experience

Far, far away, in the stars above,
There's a little planet I'm dreaming of,
I'm always wondering what could be on it,
And now I know much more than a bit!

I also am in search of creatures,
Some gooey-green ones that act like leaders,
Have you ever seen these things,
They also act like great big kings!

You see, I know a lot about them,
But they're really precious like a gem,
They also are really shiny,
But they're also really tiny...

I love being an astronaut,
You get to know a lot,
But then you start to realise
That you're in a knot!

You suddenly wake up to see you're in class,
To see your mates are in a gasp,
Then you're asking what is in their head,
They said they thought you were dead!

Kornelia Kovtun (8)
St George's Bickley CE Primary School, Bromley

Daydreaming

I'm going in search of a wizard,
I want to find him soon,
Maybe he'll make a blizzard
Or maybe a full moon
I'm going in search of a wizard,
And - is that him there?
Or is it just his lizard?
Oh no! - It's a bear!
I'm going in search of a wizard
He may be in that cave...
I really want to find him
Guess I'll just have to be brave

I turn around to see my teacher
Staring at me
She says, "Stop daydreaming and
Sit down now!"
The wizard looks at me with glee
As I say goodbye to him, I give a great big bow
I hope to see him next time
Just like now!

Georgina Johnson (8)
St George's Bickley CE Primary School, Bromley

The Fantasy Island

As I search the deadly sea
I fall and think I'm as dead as can be
But as I
Sink
I start to think
That things aren't as they seem
And I can't tell if this is a dream
I get up to see that I'm on the scene of a legend
But why do I feel threatened?
I stay still, still as can be
Until I find a herd of durdlebees!
I read it somewhere in a book
That if you even take a look
You might end up wrong
And not live for very long
So I lay down and accept my fate.

Isobel Richards (8)
St George's Bickley CE Primary School, Bromley

When It Is Night

When it is night,
My head goes off far for a flight,
In lands far, far away,
Where aliens go, "Hooray!"
Where I dream of football, pirates and birds,
Where 'dong', 'fong' and 'blong' are words,
Where paper worms are alive,
And rabbits give high fives.
And in lands further away,
The foxes are fighting at bay,
Then, I find myself in bed,
"Well, that was just a dream," I said.

Emil Kasymbekov (9)
St George's Bickley CE Primary School, Bromley

Nanna's Dogs

My nanna has two sausage dogs
They have very short legs
And when they are good
They sit down and beg.

One of them is called Mungo
He's a sausage without a bun
He likes to climb into my lap
And together we have some fun.

The other one is called Flora
She's as pesky as can be
When she gets too excited
She does a little wee!

Edie Ward (8)
St George's Bickley CE Primary School, Bromley

Roaming In Space

Last night, my dream did take flight,
In cosmic realms, bathed in starlight.
An astronaut in a suit that gleamed,
I was boarded on a celestial dream.

Through galaxies, I soared with grace,
I danced with planets, in infinite space.
Moon whispered tales untold,
As a wanderer dared to unfold.

Floating through space, weightless and free,
Planets danced in cosmic glee.
In every bit, a new story spun,
A celestial journey, just begun.

A canvas painted with colours divine,
Last night's dream was really a cosmic sign.
As an astronaut dream, I had to roam,
Exploring the space, my celestial home.

Shivam Shukla (10)
St John Vianney's Catholic Primary School, Blackpool

Monsters In The Garden

Monsters gurgling under the ground
I thought to myself, *what an awful sound*
Stomping and growling
Screaming and howling
Then I heard a noise from the bush
So I frantically ran in a rush
Looking out my window
I watched as they began to tiptoe
Sharp claws, red eyes
Surrounded by flies.
All of a sudden, they spotted me!
That's when I realised I had to flee
I watched as they came from under my bed
One of them with a big blue head
Then I woke up
And realised it was a dream
Luckily, I didn't scream!

Rebecca Bartrupe (11)
St John Vianney's Catholic Primary School, Blackpool

The Unknown World

Nothing has gotten me ready,
For the unknown world I see,
Whilst it still stands in front of me,
I see smoke and pixies,
Fly above me with flying dragons and me,
I see clouds in the shape of unicorns,
Dice in the shape of mice,
Wizards making potions,
Dogs in the bright colour blue,
But still...
A big future ahead of me!
I see stars in the sky,
It is peaceful when it's quiet,
And there in my bed,
I find myself...
It was just a dream!

Julia Foniok (11)
St John Vianney's Catholic Primary School, Blackpool

One Too Many

One night, when all lights are out,
I heard voices, almost like a shout.
There was someone in my room,
Their voice shouted like doom.
I was very scared and I wasn't prepared,
For the voice was getting closer second by second.
They said, "Tasks you must do."
And my heart grew with fear,
As the voice came near.
As it said again, "Tasks you must do,
Or something bad will happen to you."

Jack Kelly (10) & Olivia
St John Vianney's Catholic Primary School, Blackpool

The Galaxy World

Once upon a dream,
In my galaxy world,
I could see candy canes,
Chocolate grass, gingerbread houses
And marshmallow trampolines.

In my galaxy sweet world,
I made friends with unicorn angels,
Royal fairies, snowy dragons
And golden spiders that made golden silky webs.

I was exploring the magical forest,
I saw a sparkling castle,
And stairs made of diamonds,
A glamorous wizard fed me a magical stew,
It consisted of pink dust and chocolate discs with
spirals.
I became a mythical creature,
Marshmallows and chocolate lollipops in my head
called spherical hair.

I heard a voice calling me,
I woke up,
"Phew, I had a magical galaxy world dream."

Calla Bliss Rayne (8)
St Matthew's C of E Primary School, West Wimbledon

Back To London

I think about the day I said goodbye to Mum and Dad
When we thought everything was bad
The crying at the station made me very sad
Clothes and an egg sandwich in my bag is all I had

My train stop arrived and I thought I'd find someone mean
Instead, there was a family, nice and clean
They smiled and said they were the Gibbson family
But their kindness could not stop my very strange dreams

In my dream, I could go home
Back to London, where there were no bombs
Mum and Dad are happy and safe
It makes me remember my favourite place

The treehouse in our garden
It's very tall, with a ladder and is wooden
Around it, there is a low fence and a slide
With a swing beneath so you can fly

Everything feels great until I hear a scary noise
And then the screaming of the girls and boys
Everyone shouting to get inside

As the bombs rain from the sky
And Spitfires fly and fight
Into the night

I wake up and tell myself it's just a dream
And I'm safe in the country
I go to the window to see the sunrise
But then I see Spitfires fly by...

Elizabeth Worth (10)
St Matthew's C of E Primary School, West Wimbledon

Unicorn Magic

U nicorns flying in my dream

N umbers of them flying in the starry night

I feel amazed by the stars that are like a gleam

C alling my unicorn, looking left and right

O ne big fright in my dream

R ealising the unicorns are gone as I look left and right

N ot all just one unicorn stayed in this gleam

M y unicorn is about my height

A wonderful dream has ended

G one for tonight but may be back, I looked one last time

I go back to Earth, end of this gleam

C alling my unicorn to come back soon in a time.

Apolline Boursier (8)
St Matthew's C of E Primary School, West Wimbledon

I Dreamed A Smile

Once upon a dream,
I heard someone scream.
It was high-pitched and horrid,
It sounded like a little kid.

I ran to the ear-piercing noise,
The screech was made by three little boys.
Standing a metre away from them was a thrashing
bear.
They were so scared they couldn't breathe in any air.

I snapped a stick off a tree,
This was the perfect weapon and it was free.
I threw it at the growling bear,
It fainted because of the scare.
The boys ran away and disappeared into the wild,
I smiled.

Caitie Thompson (11)
St Matthew's C of E Primary School, West Wimbledon

Nightmare

N ightmares are happening, what should I do?
I think I should try and wake up.
G osh, I can't wake up, what is going to happen?
H ow do I get out of this terrible nightmare?
T ime to get my mum to get me out.
M um isn't coming, how will I get out of here?
A rgh, I'm falling! Look out for that bomb!
R evolting monsters under my bed, a giant almost
stepping on me.
E ventually, I wake up feeling safe because all my
nightmares have gone.

Edward Jarman (8)
St Matthew's C of E Primary School, West Wimbledon

Terror Devil

When you put your pyjamas on and lie in bed,
It visits every month to mess with your head.
Eyes as red as a ruby stealing your good dreams
And replacing with nightmares rudely.
Razor-sharp fangs dripping with blood,
The terrors it brings include crashing floods
And getting thrown into bubbling acid by the ones you love.
The terror devil is the thing that causes all of this,
And it came from the quantum abyss.
Crash! Bang! Open your eyes.

Kayan Bansoodeb (8)
St Matthew's C of E Primary School, West Wimbledon

Aisling

Sleep so sweet, love without a peep,
Time of day when imagination runs wild.

Aisling, Aisling, dream my dream.

Sleep, a realm undiscovered,
When true and false meet each other.

Aisling, Aisling, dream my dream.

First in bed,
Second in my faraway land.
Unicorns are walking houses,
I dream of elephants waltzing with birds.

Aisling, Aisling, dream big dreams.

Ben Grogan (11)
St Matthew's C of E Primary School, West Wimbledon

Dream

D on't look out of the window
R ead your book instead
E very window leads somewhere
A nd if you get up you will be dead
M agic comes when you are sleeping.

Sylvia Carey (8)
St Matthew's C of E Primary School, West Wimbledon

The Voices Of The Jungle

Beneath the shrubbery,
A faint chanting arose,
I knew I must hurry,
I was panting for air, hard.

I was struck with shy bladder,
Not knowing what comes next,
I could not blatter,
Or the voices would be vexed.

With worry, I turned my head,
My veins were full of dread,
For I saw a tribesman following me,
He clenched a stick in one hand a spear in the other,
I ran like never before,
I ran in and out of towering trees,
And through bushes, one and another.

I lost sight of the man of tribalisation
I had outrun him and was exhausted
Thinking about how I got there
I was also pondering
On how I could get back to civilisation

I had re-thought my life
And knew that this happening was rare

I had lost my breath and blacked out
I woke up in the hospital in a tired state
In my bed, my thoughts started to sprout
I envisioned my experience
And thought it was great
The extraordinary interaction
Shall forever be a vague mystery.

László Hüse (10)
St Thomas Of Canterbury RC Primary School, Salford

The Girl Who Flies

Once, there was a girl, her name was Levi,
I didn't know that she could fly.
I turned around, she wasn't there,
All I could do was stare.
I was beware and I looked up in the air...
Guess what? She was there!
She disappeared which was weird...
I looked around with aware,
This already seemed like a nightmare,
I shouted, "Levi,"
I felt like I was going to cry.
This is my worst fear, a tear dropped down my face,
Then I heard a voice in my ear,
Saying, "It is deadly here."
It felt like someone gave me a poke...
Levi wasn't there.
Then Levi went into the woods without fear.
She met a princess in distress, a unicorn with no horn,
trust me there was more!
Now you know there was a girl named Levi,
She could fly... No one cared!
How sad I was since I woke up and she wasn't there...

Christina Matova (9)
St Thomas Of Canterbury RC Primary School, Salford

In My Dream

In my dream every night,
I see fairies trying to say hi,
Say hi, it makes me happy
Every time.
I see sparkling stars in the sky
With my friends all the time.
My life is a cycle.
My one and only wish is to have real friends
I never said my big wish is to be a fairy
I told my last real friend and she told everyone
I ran trying to find Mom
But I realised I was all alone with my mom.
I bent down and I cried
And everyone made fun of me
And that is why I don't have a real friend
Only in my dream.

Iwinosa Gabbrellia (8)
St Thomas Of Canterbury RC Primary School, Salford

Save Planet Earth!

I am the Earth
And the Earth is me
Look at how I'm suffering

Ban the bomb!
Save the whale!
Please don't step on
That poor snail.

Why waste half your dinner?
Why discard your tea?
Why throw anything away
Just because it's free?

Recycle your waste
Throw nothing away
It'll come in useful
One fine rainy May.

That's why we celebrate this day
That's why across the world we say.

As long as life,
As clear as free

I am the Earth
And the Earth is me.

Horiya Azid (8)
St Thomas Of Canterbury RC Primary School, Salford

Marc's Crazy Dream

Once upon a time,
There was a boy named Marc,
He tried to go to sleep
And everything slowly went dark.
He woke in a dream
Which was very fun,
Until the nightmare had begun.
Everyone stopped in fear,
Then tears started to appear
Marc was cornered
By monsters,
He was petrified
Until the dark came light and
Everything was fine.
The next day
Marc went to sleep
Where he dreamt of a
Wonderland
It was so fun
So very fun
It was just right!

Dexter Obasogie (9)
St Thomas Of Canterbury RC Primary School, Salford

Dancing Teachers

In my dreams every night
Dancing teachers groove with colours bright
Vibrant colours and spinning feet
One by one they click to the beat
The lead dancers linger along the floor
And the backup ones spin like never before
From a distant planet far beyond
They've come to Earth to make a bond
Every night I leave out shoes
Hoping I'll make them stay
But sadly, they just disappear
For now, until perhaps next year.

Hannan Albath (10)
St Thomas Of Canterbury RC Primary School, Salford

All The Creatures

In a land where colours shine so bright
Meet the creatures, a magical sight.
Wobbly giggles, wiggle, a rainbow dance.
Tiny paws and playful prance.
Snuggle snatch in trees so tall
Whispers secret to all, Fluffernix soars with
Wings ablaze, spreading warmth with magic rays
Creatures dance, wild and free
Imagination's magic, pure and sweet
This all happened in my dreams
A place where all is possible.

Thomas Donley (9)
St Thomas Of Canterbury RC Primary School, Salford

A Thousand Dreams

A thousand dreams
Some are big
Others just small
We never know
If they could grow tall.

Sometimes we get lost
Sometimes we don't
We never know
We might turn into frost.

We might be builders
We might be astronauts
Who knows
We might be in everyone's thoughts

A thousand dreams
Floating around
We never know what will happen
When we open our eyes.

Samina Haji (10)
St Thomas Of Canterbury RC Primary School, Salford

Seasons

There are so many reasons,
Why I love seasons,
I love spring,
The flowers it brings,
I love summer,
So many newcomers,
I love autumn,
The days don't shorten,
I love winter,
There are barely any sprinters,
There are so many reasons,
To love seasons,
You better not run,
Because I've only just begun!
There are so many reasons,
To love the seasons.

Ayat Uddin (9)
St Thomas Of Canterbury RC Primary School, Salford

Dream Job

D ream I'm dreaming about is so extreme,
R eally excited about this new thing,
E agerly it starts at 8:05 but I want it at 7:05,
A dmitting this job will be so fun,
M y excitement makes me happier than ever.

J obs are boring but not this one,
O r they sometimes can be good,
B ut don't explode because you can get detention!

Lana Khoshnaw (8)
St Thomas Of Canterbury RC Primary School, Salford

Regrets

Rude things you say
Everything you say or do is mean but you don't mean it
Goodness comes back to you
Regrets on what you said or did
Tell them sorry but they don't believe you
Seriously I am you say but they say go away, now you
have lost someone very close, either they come back or
they are gone forever.

Therese Mendy (8)
St Thomas Of Canterbury RC Primary School, Salford

Why?

Why shine a torch for light, if it's already bright?
Why look for treasure if there's none?
Why have fun if you feel numb?
If the sky is blue, does that mean you have to turn blue too?
Why be a girl if you can't twirl?
Why?
Why?
Why?
Why?
Why?
Why?

Sharon Eze (9)
St Thomas Of Canterbury RC Primary School, Salford

The Night I Dream

The night I dream,
I see a different world ahead of me!
I see a magical world with fairies and elves.
With lovely flowers and beautiful trees
It feels good
It feels fun, but what can be ahead of me?
It is fun here with the fairies and elves
But a happy day is waiting for me!

Elim Frezgi (9)
St Thomas Of Canterbury RC Primary School, Salford